The Paper Rose

Tom Absher

Plain View Press
P. O. 42255
Austin, TX 78704

plainviewpress.net
sb@plainviewpress.net
1-512-441-2452

Copyright Tom Absher, 2007. All rights reserved.
ISBN: 978-1-891386-83-1
Library of Congress Number: 2007929653

Acknowledegements

Poems in this collection which appeared previously in poetry journals:

"Language of the Garden," *Icarus*; "Chelsea," *Hunger Mountain Review*; "Animals," *The Country Journal*; "A Parent's Death," *Poet Lore;* "V-E Day," *The Writer's Voice*; "Where do animals go when the time has come to die?" *Nimrod*; "Grace," "My Conscientious Objection," *The Cafe Review*; "Beth Israel 2 AM," "Mrs. Townsend," *Sheila-na-gig*; "Patient Murray" "Tree of Life," *Texas Observer*; "Newsreel," *Witness*; "The Sheep," *Goddard Journal*.

Contents

I   War Child   7

War Child	9
Tinfoil	11
The Hornet	13
World War Two	14
V-E Day	16
The Horn	17
The Sheep	18
Tree of Life	20
Carousel	22
Newsreel	23
The Museum of Tolerance	24
War Math	26

II   Alternative Service   29

Jamie and Tommy	31
My Conscientious Objection	33
Where You Are	34
Altar Boy	36
Alternative Service	37
The Hospital	39
Patient Murray	40
The Caul	41
Beth Israel, 2AM	42
Death Rattle	44
Mrs. Townsend	45
Brought Back	47

III   Vanishing Animal   49

Animals	51
Zoo	52
The Feather	54
Farm Cat	55

	Language of the Garden	56
	Noah	57
	Abraham	58
	The Desert	59
	The Salamander	61
	Night Sky	62
	Where do animals go when the time has come to die?	64
IV	**Paper Rose**	**65**
	Paper Rose	67
	Circus	69
	The Veil	71
	All Souls Day, November First	72
	Marriage Poem	74
	Snapshot	75
	A Parent's Death	76
	Mother's Wish	77
	Chelsea	78
	Grace	79
	The Dream of the Pavilion	80
	Notes	81
	About the Author	83

For Robin, Shannon, Matthew, and Erika,
who are everything in my life

I
War Child

War Child

Even as I was first tasting
the fragrant air coming off
wheat fields of the central plains
and having a look-see
at the small town worlds in Kansas,
and Illinois —
Europe and Asia
had drawn open the curtain:
Act One, World War II.

In Matoon, Illinois,
we lived in a wood-frame house
nicknamed the Coal Smoke House
because sitting so close
to the railroad tracks
it had turned shades of charcoal
from the smoke and coal dust
spewing off
the steam engines of the trains
my dad worked for
and I loved at first sight and sound.

The Santa Fe, the Union Pacific,
the Illinois Central and the Baltimore and Ohio
rattled window panes, china cups,
and our very bones
with the glorious — to me —
hard-charging, world-consuming racket
they made with their smoke-pluming,
fire-eating, eight master-wheel
engine ferociousness.

To the very small, massive engines
and screaming whistles
make for dragon heads

on long reptile bodies of passenger cars,
or freight and tanker cars
and whether they were coming or going,
day or night, these trains ate
peace and quiet for breakfast,
lunch and dinner.

And as I stood in our yard
and waved at the engineer,
fireman, and caboose-man,
all across the globe
boilers had been fired
for the dragon-breathed
war-trains of Nanking, Guernica,
Sudetenland and the Kristallnacht Express,
and they were consuming cities
and villages and houses
and transporting people in boxcars
to death camps
in a steam-whistle scream
of fire, black smoke and human dust:

All aboard.

Tinfoil

Grandmother taught us to save tinfoil
for the war effort by wrapping it into balls.
It was 1943 and I was five; it was something
I could do. There was a song on the radio:
Praise the Lord and pass the Ammunition,
which I sang as: *Praise the Lord
and pass the Tinfoil Balls.*

Our parents smoked, so cigarette packs
were available for the archaeology
of separating out the foil liners, adding
them to balls which grew into rough-faced,
shiny moons.

The street, playgrounds, vacant lots,
I scoured the world for metallic paper,
and when the balls became softball size
I took them to the collection station
behind the grocery store. I felt I was
helping the fight against Hitler, a monster.

With his storm troops in their brown shirts,
his goose-stepping army, his hysterical voice,
Hitler grew more monstrous in my dreams
and my parents' dreams. Listening to his ranting
on the radio as she ironed, Mother once said
out loud: *I wish someone would eliminate that man.*

I daydreamed how I might save enough
of the tinfoil balls to make a sword of silver
and kill Hitler myself, personally, as he sat
at his desk beneath the black swastika.

I had heard stories in which magic swords,
with personalities and their own names,

were used for slaying dragons, swords made
from metal mined in caves by trolls.

But for me, a boy from Texas intent on saving
the world and obeying his mother's wishes,
a sword forged from tinfoil glowing in spheres
on my dresser in the moonlight, spheres
I had created myself,
such a home-made sword would have to do.

The Hornet

Inside a wooden matchbox
I kept a dead, perfectly preserved
brown, paper wasp
that had died in our Chevy,
bested in a struggle
with the rear window.

I studied the wasp's
propeller shaped wings
with a magnifying glass:
road maps of lace and capillaries,
church windows made
of gauze, tapered and filigreed
for flight and the viola strum
of hornet music.

Here was a miniaturized
B-17 *Flying Fortress*
poised for take off, an insect angel
with a black abdomen,
devoted to making houses
of hexagonal chambers, tiered
with paper and hung
from a stem under eaves.

When this hornet lived
no one could tell me
that it did not sense its beauty
and power, and when it flew
that it did not glory
in the roar of its wings.

World War Two

Each week *Life* magazine arrived
bringing war stories, photos
and maps with little flags
stuck on countries
proclaiming allegiances.
Everybody on the globe
was at war with somebody.

The flags looked like name-cards
at the Mad Hatter's tea party
except the Hatter, the March Hare,
and the Dormouse were armed,
and so was Alice.

My brother and I grew up
in the midst of this war
with its gasoline rationing,
victory gardens, collecting scrap
metal, the universal shortage
of bubble gum, and Hitler-hating.
On the radio we had heard a tape recording
of *der Fuhrer* giving a mad, ranting speech.
He was easy to hate, easy to fear.

Wearing plastic Army helmets,
Army patches sewed on our jackets
by mother, we played soldier daily
and called each other Joe.
When a polio outbreak
closed our school,
our parents put us on the train
by ourselves to summer camp
in Michigan. It reminded me
of newsreels showing British children
boarding trains to the country side
fleeing London's bombing raids.

Dad gave the porter money
to look after us. We were too excited
to be worried because the Pullman cars
were filled with soldiers, going off
to war, or home on leave.

In khaki uniforms, dog tags,
close cropped hair, endless smoking
and rough language, they embodied heroism
and to us were gods.

We were speechless as we
absorbed them: their jokes, laughter,
gestures, the way they kept packs
of cigarettes in their socks, tucked
army caps in their belts. One guy
walked-the-dog with his yo-yo
up and down the aisle.

At times, watching the landscape
unroll through Texas into Oklahoma,
their faces grew quiet and distant.

Observing the wartime blackout,
in the evening, the conductors and porters
pulled down all the shades in the train.
When it slowed passing through
small towns, the crossing bells
ding-ding-dinging,
cars were there waiting,
going places — families out for a movie,
a couple on a date. Everyone stared
at the shrouded train, its single headlamp
blazing forward into the darkness.

V-E Day

World War II ended in the summer
of 1945 and Mr. Coles, the camp director
came to our cabin to announce it.
The war is over, he said, and then
he sat down and wept in front of us,
a big barrel of a man, his huge hands
covering his face.

A photograph of Mr. Cole's son
hung in the hall of the dining room
with a black ribbon across one corner —
a boy in uniform killed on Omaha beach
on D-Day.

Mr. Coles went to the veranda
of the dining hall and dragged
the big ship's bell used to call
boys to meals down to the shore
of the lake and there he rang the bell —
BONG BONG BONG BONG BONG.

He banged the bell long after
we had all come to dinner,
he banged it through the meal,
disturbing everyone, even the grownups,
extending the sound-barrage

as each new peal piled up
on the one before it,
BONG BONG BONG BONG BONG
fusing the sound into one continuous clamor,
an invisible vibration arcing
over the lake and out into space.

The Horn

In the camp crafts shop
I made a horn out of papier mache
and silver wrapping paper,
rolled and tapered
into a slender cone.
Slathered over with glue
it took on an archaic,
biblical look.

The horn was meant to be
for celebrating V-E day.
When I blew on it, all it would do
was make the mournful sound
of someone playing a bugle
who doesn't know how to play
a bugle. But I was glad
it made any sound at all.

Later one night in a dream, I walked
into a clearing and blew the horn's
wounded call, once, twice, three times.
Slowly, animals appeared
at the edge of the woods.
I could make out silhouettes of deer,
rabbits, horses, elephants,
and giraffes.

They stood keeping their distance
as I blew more of the horn's
feathery notes, long and low
into the darkness.
Curious, patient, watching me
they never moved as they listened.
I knew they had come to comfort
all of us.

The Sheep

A flock of sheep and spring lambs
grazing on the sweet carpet grass
at our camp at the lake,
resembled a collection of wind-up toys:
heads down, tails wagging, droppings
falling as they inched along. My father
had warned our neighbor to keep
his sheep fenced or he would shoot them.
Father only warned you once.

He put the car in park
and turned off the engine. No one
said a word as he stepped out,
opened the trunk and selected
a rifle. Using the door for a brace,
he drew a bead and began popping
the animals down with the .22
and they fell and ran and stumbled
toward the break in the fence
and he shot more as they climbed
over each other.

When the rifle was spent
of its twelve rounds,
the yard was lumpy with dead
and dying sheep. He ordered
my brother and me to drag them
off the property. A few flies
had already found the blood.
Grabbing the creatures
by their legs we carried them
through the fence and into a pile.
It was most awful handling the lambs.

We repaired the fence
and came back to the house.
We never spoke of it then or afterwards.
Early on, we had learned that
talking only makes bad things worse
by making them real.

That evening at dinner,
like four people descending
the ocean's deepest trench
in a bathysphere, our family silence
grew in magnitude, as if
we each knew that at such depths
speech was a waste
of what little oxygen we had left.

Tree of Life

When I caught my first trout,
cleaned, cooked, and ate it with my father
next to a stream in Colorado,
I remember fingering the delicate lace
of bones joining head to tail,
that soft, white tree upon which
the fish had hung its life.

In military school
when it rained they showed us
World War II training films:
How to Recognize Syphilis,
How to Dig a Foxhole, and
How to Be a Sniper — meaning
which enemy soldier do you shoot first
in order to kill the other two
before they run
when all three are walking single file
in an open field.

My long descent into disastrous trouble
with my draft board, the F.B.I., the Justice
Department, and my family and friends,
had its seed planting that rainy afternoon
as I watched the cross hairs
of the sniper's rifle enclose
each enemy soldier's head
and explode it.

Enemy soldier.

An eighth grader, I was
too young to fully grasp the concept,
and could only imagine each man
as someone like me, a kid, his youth

unlived, his best stories still
waiting for him up ahead
in that field, or hidden in the branches
of the tree of bones growing
inside him.

Carousel

Many German prisoners of war
were held in the U.S.
and the military bases in San Antonio
got their share. Those who had
the skills were given work
carving wooden horses
for the carousel at Playland,
the city's amusement park.

I remember loving to ride
those fiery wooden steeds as a child —
with their multicolored saddles,
bridles, reins, and stirrups,
their open-mouths gulping air
as they laid bare their big teeth,
tossed their heads and manes
in an ecstasy of frozen-in-motion
wildness.

Enemy prisoners of war making
fantasy horses for a merry-go-round
I rode as a child — what if
they had never made
How to Be a Sniper
training films and one or more
enemy soldiers got away,
were captured, sent to a POW camp
in Texas and there carved galloping,
cavorting, ecstatically energetic horses
in a stampede of freedom for their
imagination and mine — what then?

Newsreel

Again those images come back.
In some old footage on ETV
World War II is over, the allies
are liberating the death camps.
Everything is in black and white —
it is impossible to imagine color.
The voice-over tells us the Nazis
are being made to bury the dead
and to carry away the living dead.
A figure drags a body to a mass grave,
but it is not a body anymore,
it is a bundle of human limbs.
He heaves the bundle into the hole
where its limbs flail in a cartwheel
of X's: X X X until it lands
on the pile at the bottom.
Out of all the scenes like this
I have watched, this was the one
I was meant to see, this one
will be mine to remember.

The Holocaust has given us
a new way of measuring human response:
since nothing we do in its memory
can touch it, anything we do in its memory
is of value. From a list of the known dead
at Treblinka I have chosen a name
to give to the X. Any would serve,
there were so many. I might give
the X my own name because
probably all our names appear somewhere
among the millions and millions.
From time to time I speak the name
from the list: *Johann Sturzer*.

The Museum of Tolerance

Each visitor to the Holocaust exhibit
receives an I.D. card
for someone who was a victim
of the Final Solution.

My card was for Bronislaw Honig,
a boy about my age in 1943,
who even resembled me in his photo
wearing a sailor suit like the one I had.
He was born in Cracow, I in Kansas —
my double from within the mirror
of fate, omen of the dead.

To prevent his being sent
to the death camp at Belzec,
Bronislaw's father hid his son
in a suitcase which he carried to a cart
piled with bags left behind by the Jews.
Mr. Honig asked a Christian woman
to smuggle Bronislaw away.
Later the woman and the boy were discovered,
arrested and murdered.

I have kept the print-out,
a page about Bronislaw's life,
and his photo in the sailor suit,
so I can take it out and look at him.
The suitcase I will have to imagine,
myself the father of a boy - finding one
large enough to hold my son,
making air holes in it, squeezing him in,
closing it up, fastening the straps,
speaking to my Matthew in whispers,
urging him not to cry, to be brave.
But my son packed like a fetus

in darkness and leather, the awkward way
of carrying the suitcase
so it would not look heavy, carrying it
as gently as possible to comfort him,
then leaving him on a wagon alone forever —
this I cannot imagine.

War Math

When you're in warrior training
learning how to kill an enemy soldier,
remember to steep yourself
in the study of Advanced Subtraction.

First, subtract the man
from his mother and father
who carried him in their arms
of love and patience
into his adulthood;
subtract from them their hearts
at their son's military funeral
where they exchange their lives
for the folded flag from his coffin
that his mother will clutch to her breast
while his father stares into the emptiness
of the middle distance,
now his private room, his assigned cell
to the end of his days.

Next, subtract from the man
his wife, her face full of light for him,
subtract forever that light between them;
subtract his young son, already with a trace
of his father's demeanor
about the nose and eyes,
subtract from the boy's entire life
the holy need of his father's presence
and example and approval;
subtract the daughters and sons planned
yet unborn; subtract his tribal community
of family, relatives, and friends —
those people who now realize
how much they knew themselves
by knowing him.

To kill another soldier
remember to subtract from him
the twelve volume encyclopedia
of his night and day dreams
over a lifetime, that impenetrable
cabalistic text of image and mystery
unfolding the richness of his double,
triple, quadruple selves, and subtract
from the man (and this perhaps
is the highest mathematics of all)
his own death, his *private* death,
the death he would have met
had he lived out his allotted life,
that unique destiny
set in motion at birth, in his stars,
his cells.

When you have the enemy
in the cross hairs of your sights
and pulling the trigger is not
going to be an option,
make certain you have done
the math.

II
Alternative Service

Jamie and Tommy

We were boon companions.
I lived on Devine Road and he on Ironwood
but our houses were connected by a footpath,
our very own Santa Fe Trail
across two vacant lots.
After years and thousands of hours
in each other's company,
we learned to live in unison —
like those guys in old vaudeville acts
who walked across the stage together
inside one pair of pants.

Depending on the changing menu at his house
or mine, we took our meals together,
eating in sync, the same number of black-eyed peas
on our forks. We drank jointly
from faucets, using our hands the way Tarzan did,
folded like two leaves into a cup,
the water running down our chins. So,
when we had to pee at the same time
and stepped outside to write our signatures
in the dirt, making an overlapping monogram
of our single lifeline,
we took it as a sign we were brothers.

As early as first grade, Jamie and I
wished to be Superman. Stripped to underpants,
bath towels pinned at our necks,
we raced from the back of my brother's room
through a hallway into my room
onto the second floor landing
and leapt at my father's door —
arms outstretched like Superman's —
falling on the big bed.

We repeated this routine all afternoon,
dashing through the empty house
like midgets crazed on comic books.
Since we had the same blood
we promised that if one ever flew,
the other would share the power.

Jamie died in a car crash at sixteen.
Whenever I visit the cemetery
and stand at the foot of his grave,
my soul has to strain hard to do the work
for both of us. It lifts off the ground heavily,
rising slowly over rooftops into the sky,
a sky containing a cow and some flowers
perhaps a moon — our one soul ascending
like two Chagall lovers
separate and joined forever.

My Conscientious Objection

Jamie's death was at the root of it.
He was killed at sixteen rolling his father's
four-door Ford off the blacktop
and when he died I didn't believe it
for a year. I tried to keep him alive
pretending I'd see him again.
How could he be dead
if he still lived inside me?

Killing another guy, a soldier, would mean
killing him in so many other people,
for the rest of their lives. Like me
they wouldn't believe it and would go on
trying to keep him alive inside them.

When one death arrives, it takes down
whole families, communities. Like life
stuck in reverse, death just keeps on dying
and never stops dying, knocking down
one person after another.

I didn't want to kill another person,
nor did I want to be taught how.
This is what I wanted to tell my draft board:

I refuse to enter military service
because for ten years my best friend
and I were like one person and he died
and I still love him. I'll do something else
to serve my country. One death is enough for me.

Where You Are

One ordinary day
in the young life he was living
Jamie was alive, present,
he was my childhood friend-for-life,
the one who in our old age
would recall with me
our childhood together. Then
on another ordinary day
he was killed in a car wreck
and was buried and gone.

Many times
I drove to visit his grave,
to stand on the grass
beneath which is his coffin,
in which his body lies in a suit
he never owned and
would never have worn in life.

I spoke to him in my mind,
my heart, words pouring down
from the soles of my feet into
his grave. After decades,
still shock, the old loss.

One day a response
grew in me forcefully,
with painful simplicity:

I have crossed over.
You are still there, on your side.
Your time will come and you will
cross over. While you can,
every day, even as you walk
back to your car, even sipping

your morning cup of coffee,
cherish being alive, give it
all you've got being
where you are.

Altar Boy

What did they think?
Training me to assist the priest
inside the altar rail, handling
the chalice, the ciborium,
then the water, the wine, and the Host,
a sou-chef working with
the Head Chef in the kitchen
of transubstantiation.

On that side of the rail,
I was in the aura of the cross,
I lit the candles before Mass
and put them out after,
I carried the tall cross
up the central aisle which
signaled the parishioners to bow
their heads. I helped the priest
serve the body and blood of Christ
to my parents, kneeling at the altar rail
like children.

Did they think I would not be affected
by God's smell in the beeswax candles,
God's voice in the words spoken
at the altar, God's presence in the
bread and wine? I was initiated
into these mysteries and the mysteries
initiated me back.

So when the time came to join the military
to learn to kill the enemy, why was everyone
so shocked I chose the longer,
more hopeless path? Did it never occur to anyone
that the alchemist's apprentice
might be changed too?

Alternative Service

After a twoyear struggle with
the Justice Department, the FBI,
and various legal advisors,
my draft board ordered me
to serve the country as an orderly
in a hospital. I was as pleased to do it
as they were to be rid of me.

We orderlies wore brown smocks
like druggists-in-training,
got beeper calls to do odd jobs
throughout the hospital,
but mostly we prepared the dead
for the morgue. For someone
who did not want to learn to kill,
learning to work with the dead
was an irony not lost on me.

After the deceased's family left
with the priest or rabbi, two of us
would enter the room, stagehands
preparing the strike the set
after the sacred drama.

We rolled the body onto a gauzy shroud,
stoppered its orifices with cotton balls,
tied hands and feet with cloth strips:
arms crossed for Christians, down
at the sides for Jews; a ribbon closed
the jaw and the name tag went on a big toe.

Tying both ends of the shroud
like a package, we delivered it
to the morgue on a gurney, selecting
a pull-out tray from the wailing wall

of steel doors. I often thought, one day
someone like me will do these things
to my body and I began to carry
my own death in me like a charm.

I never got over the shock
of being so close to the dead —
it felt holy to me. We lowly orderlies
were like rogue priests,
doing the dirty work of the sacred.
My hands can still recall
the cool feel of the dead,
that soft heaviness,
the way a body seems to resist
being rolled into the shroud.

I got so when I walked home
I could picture how people
on the street would look
when their time comes.
Entering our apartment from
the graveyard shift, I watched
my wife stir in her sleep, then
slowly waken, like a princess
in a fairy tale, the fairy tale
of being among the living.

The Hospital

I came to love the building.
So much that went on inside
was not of this world —
the *this world* of the street
and my everyday life.

There were two old men
who operated a roasted chestnut cart
out front. They had gnarly,
wizened European faces
from some black and white footage
of World War II survivors:
the long, dusky overcoats,
old fashioned caps, shoes
from God knows what century.
No one knew where
they were from, what language
they spoke.

I thought of them as gatekeepers,
marking the entrance
to the looming building
with its allegorical levels: top floors
for childbirth, basement for the morgue,
Dante's tiers of Hell and Purgatory
everywhere else.

The steam whistle of their shiny,
stainless steel wagon
made the strident announcement:

Out here is the street. In there
is something else. Check
your metaphysical books at the door
and remember to wipe your shoes.

Patient Murray

In the recovery room next to the O.R.
where patients, post-surgery,
waited in big metal beds, their
sidebars raised, surrounded
by oxygen tanks, I.V. poles, life-support
monitors in a jumble of tubes
and wires and beeping machines,
a woman surfaced from the sea
of her anesthesia. She began
breathing hard, one breath climbing
to the next as if she was preparing
to dive back down, then she opened
her eyes for one last look
and died. The beeping stopped.

Matter-of-factly, someone said:
Patient Murray went out
(*went out* being hospital code for *died*)
and nurses and interns began
to disconnect her from the mechanical
trees of life canopying her bed.
It was my first eye witness to a death,
and I thought everyone should slow down
so something more in keeping could happen
some grace, some courtesy, a pause
so her soul, its long work completed
might find its way out of the body
at its own pace, with dignity, like an elder.

The Caul

They kept your mother
flat on her back for seven months,
out of fear of losing you
through her weakened cervix.

And when the birthing moment
arrived in the eighth month
you slid so quickly from her body
the nurse only had time
to catch you in her open hands
like a piece of fruit tumbling
from the tree by its own weight.

There was silence
at the end of the bed.
Your mother asked: *What is it?
What is wrong with my baby?*
and she showed you to her,
how your face was still covered
by the amniotic membrane
from the birth sac, the caul,
attached at the hairline like
a fleshy veil.

When the nurse lifted it,
translucent, moist,
it made a perfect life-mask:
sculpted nose, mouth, cheekbones —
a soft replica of your face
that kept about it a look of wonder.
Your mother made the sign
of the cross and as she received you
with your little mask, she announced:
Blessed be, it is the face of the soul.

Beth Israel, 2AM

A woman was delivered
of her stillborn baby girl
on my night shift. The child
had been carefully wrapped
in an infant's blanket, fastened
with a large safety pin
nearly as big as the bundle.

I placed it on the gurney
for the short ride to the elevator
down to the basement catacombs
and the morgue.

A nurse accompanied me —
we made a solemn procession:
a silent, stricken honor guard
for a tender loaf.

Moving through the darkened hospital,
feeling self-conscious, vaguely embarrassed
to be among the living, to have greedily
had so much life already,
I gave up worrying about who I was,
or who God was, or any thoughts
about what I had to lose
by beseeching God

for some blessing
on this child who had known nothing,
not even the pleasure of one breath.

Comfort her, comfort her.

And as I steered the long gurney,
its wobbly right front wheel
made a squeaky echoing music
as if to mock me, my prayer, and
the solemn ritual.

So be it.

Death Rattle

Mr. La Perle's heart stopped
at 12:45 AM, the other
vital signs flat-lined,
and they laid him on the floor
trying to resuscitate him
with the heel of a hand.

I was called at 1 AM
to bring a shroud-bag
to the room where the body
was lying on the floor
under a sheet.

As I cranked down the bed
to put him on it and do my work,
his body finished dying
by expelling the last air
from his lungs,
up the windpipe and out.

The gurgling, clearing-the-throat
sound was delivered slowly
in a deep, living voice — as if
the body was saying its goodbye.

On nights like these,
terrified I would die from
my own heart attack,
I wished I had gone into the army.

Mrs. Townsend

In the autopsy room
Mrs. Townsend was sitting up
as if she were in bed,
except she was unclothed
and on a stainless steel table,
her skull and chest
rudely opened up
like packages at customs.

Two men in rubber aprons
and gloves, busied themselves
around her, one removing the brain,
cradling it in his hands like a crown,
the other scooping organs
from the body's big cavity
into a great metal bowl —
like a pirate digging doubloons
out of the sand.

I had been called to transfer
a cadaver to the morgue
and stood transfixed by the sight
of this older woman, a patient
I had come to know slightly,
having her inner cosmos
with all its gleaming shapes
removed from her body.

I was violating a taboo
by looking at an elderly woman
undressed and the greater violation
of seeing her body's treasures
being separated from each other
one by one:

the body's solar deity, the brain,
a ball of dough on a tray, the liver,
angular, dark as Neptune, her intestinal
Saturn-like rings in a jumble,
the gibbous heart-moon
looking forlorn in a jar of fluid.

Her organs set free,
isolated, useless, yet each one
magnificent to see
and marvel at — I could not
take my eyes away —
because they are the ones
in all of us, those ignored
gatherings of inner planets
whose quietly dutiful work
keeps us alive.

Finally the men began
stuffing the cavities
of her skull and torso
with handfuls of unwoven rope:
oakum — a word which still
makes me shudder — to give
her body's emptiness
the illusion of shape and grace.

Brought Back

When we got the STAT call
to bring oxygen to Seven North
the two of us ran down the halls,
pushing hand trucks with oxygen tanks,
their hoses, masks, wrenches clanking
and bouncing as if we were in a comic
race at the hospital staff picnic.

The patient was lying on the floor,
her skin overcast
like Boston's winter sky
before a snow storm. I held
the goose-necked lamp from
her bedside table while an intern,
the only doctor present
who had done a thoracotomy,
untied her gown, gently lifted
the curve of her breast
and made a deep incision
into the rib cage.

With the separators he opened
the ribs and rolled up his sleeve
preparing to place a gloved hand
on the stopped heart — all done
carefully, almost in slow motion,
reminding me of the time I watched
firefighters just on the scene
of a raging fire in New York
go through their methodical,
choreographed dance of unfolding,
laying out of hoses, now positioning
the ladders — *all of it adagio:*
This is life and death, do not rush —

and up to the wrist the hand reached
down past skin and bone into the cavity
of the heart, the body's treasure room,
searching for a grip on this woman's
vanishing life as she tumbled, fell,
spiraled into the Abyss —

the hand extending after one flailing
leg, an ankle, catching it, now firmly
holding on, slowly pulling her whole self
back out of the darkness, the body
its color changing to the early light
of dawn, spreading a faint tinge of rose
over the snow covered city.

III
Vanishing Animal

Animals

Coming back from a walk
with the dogs, I find
ten deer beds beneath
the apple trees. At night,
heavy from summer feeding,
they imprint the grass deeply
with their sleeping bodies.

Later that evening
I take the compost bucket
to empty it on the garden
and I can hear deer noises
in the orchard. I shine
my light toward the trees
but its beam doesn't reach.

Standing in the dark,
listening, I imagine clusters,
whole families of deer
chewing apples, looking
into the darkness where the light was
imagining me as they eat —

all of us joined for a moment
by our invisible lives.

Zoo

Each animal here
is a darkening poem
in a doomsday book, each
poem-animal has its title
and for so many
the same epigraph:

Sumatran Tiger, Vanishing Animal
American Bald Eagle, Vanishing Animal
Siberian Snow Leopard, Vanishing Animal

It is a long list
and the analogy is unavoidable:
Death Row.

Watch the tiger, the spotted
panthers, see their eyes
opening, giving form
to shape — next time
they may be gone.

We can scarcely take in
these works of art anymore,
having lost the courage
to look other creatures
in the eye in silence.

A sign here should read:

Do not feed the animals.
Do not tap on the glass.
Do not speak of them
in their presence. Look
them in the eye and if
they look back, endure it.

*Say nothing. Go and carry
away inside you as many
animals as you can.
It is your only hope.
It is their only escape.*

The Feather

Do not make the mistake
of studying alchemy
before you have studied
the one feather left in your yard
by a raven, maybe left there
just for you, one among
the many hundreds which
enclose the raven in a glossy panoply
of pitch black, iridescent blue,
green and purple,
all the feathers joining together
to make and win
their plumage argument with gravity
for ascent, flight, for soaring, wafting,
becoming airborne and staying airborne,
wing beat after wing beat
each feather a miracle of design and beauty
whether a primary, secondary,
or contour quill
from a wing or a tail,
or a downy feather
from the inner coat of the raven's
dark breast; do not search
for the philosopher's stone
until you have studied this feather closely
imagining where it has been, what
it has seen, the part it has played
working in silence high over the earth,
lofting the raven up with the thermals
to glide and drift as if it were
finding its way toward heaven.

Farm Cat

Our old Tom
spends his days
in the quiet zones
of the empty barn.

Always by himself,
he lounges on a beam
half-sleeping, half-studying
a working spider.

He will sit for hours,
poised in the door
of a shed, a hunter —
semi-retired — watching
the morning make its moves.

When sunlight silvers
the tips of his fur,
a neighbor's two black labs
run the ridge of the hill,
noisy, rambunctious, in pursuit.

Attentively, his eyes
rheumy, ears notched
from the wars,
Tommy takes them in,
calculating the distance,
their intentions.

Everything is what it is
and they too are part of it.

Language of the Garden

Before Eve, before Adam got help,
he was alone with the animals
who had no names. Some
were as loose-limbed and formless
as clouds over water, playfully
exchanging shapes, becoming swan-like,
taking sheep outlines, imitating
bird sounds, mammal noises
while awaiting their names
and fixed forms.

In his youth, Adam was bilingual,
fluent in the language of the garden
and spirit-speak, a laughing-in-tongues,
the sounds of an exotic jungle bird
as yet unnamed, singing in the trees,
asking to be noticed.

When my neighbor Robert gathers in
his draft horses, he calls to them
with made-up words, animal sounds
for *home* and *dinner*.
Adam would have approved.

At night walking through his barn
checking on the cows, quiet
in beds of straw except for their
moist breathing, Adam talks
to them, as he thinks up
how best to name them.
Each one nestled down on herself,
eating and re-chewing, lost
in her thoughts making milk —
the cows are content to wait.
They already know who they are.

Noah

At night, snug in his berth
deep in the chambers of the ark,
when the shipboard menagerie
is quiet, asleep in the gentle
motions of the gopher wood cradle,

Noah hears music beneath the hull,
faintly at first, then a growing
chorus of sluicing leviathans,
whales, dolphins —
chanting lamentations for all
the creatures lost in the rising waters.

He imagines groupings of sea-beasts
swimming in amongst drowned cities,
towns, villages, passing through rooms
and windows into wavy streets
plaintively sighing in watery tones
like ghosts — *everything gone,
everyone gone.*

Noah thinks of his home, the warm
work room with his books, carpentry tools,
plants drying, his wife's garden,
the big oak in the yard and all their animals
left behind: the working dogs, the barn
with its sheep, goats, cows —

and when he recalls leaving
their many beloved house cats,
sitting in the front window
watching, puzzled that they
are being left behind,
his soul begins its own painful song,
joining the music of the sea below.

Abraham

At home in the atoms
of the invisible and unspeakable,
he taught himself the art
of listening, as do poets, monks,
witches, and magicians,
wandering in silence,
exercising their powers.

West from Ur and the Euphrates
he wandered into the desert,
absorbing its soft shapes,
its pure white skeletons
of animals, the glass silence
presiding over everything
with no beginning or end.

As he grew older he ventured
more deeply into the prism
of absence, listening his way
down through its layers.

Abraham trekked so far
he arrived at a place
where cuneiform letters
danced in the air, soundlessly,
a scattering of dark birds
spelling out his mission
and his fate.

The Desert

Many people have walked
into one desert or another
to find their gods, like Arabia,
east of the Euphrates, an unholy
violence of heat, sand, and those
salamanders which thrive
on fire from the sun, because
there is so little else to eat.

If one seeks to hear the voice
of a deity it might be found there,
where sky overwhelms the land,
where there is no sound
but the pulse of blood in the ear.

It has been said that divinity
does not speak in thunder clouds
or a whirlwind, or from the bottom
of a well, but in the presence
of animals, or the voice of a child,
ordinary, soft-spoken words, sounds,
musings, a question,
a voice so small one must go
into the desert to hear it,
to believe it.

I have heard it is a voice
that addresses us everyday
in one form or another,
but we never notice,
perhaps like the voice Abraham heard
before he set out for the Promised Land,
that place overrunning with milk and honey
and war, endless war —

words first heard so faintly
so close by, he might have thought
they were from the salamander
beneath his feet:

Return here often and listen for me.

The Salamander

*Are you surprised
to hear me speak?
Small dragon on sticky feet,
wearing the mask of a god,
a creature of light
I also live on darkness,
within earshot of the pulse
of your heart. I know
this desert well,
its rocky outcrops, their
reptilian crevices,
opening and closing
with the sun, its solar
ebbs and flows.*

*I am a hermit among
the crags, I know my body
as my house — do you
know yours as well?
Have you made your peace
with it? Said your goodbyes,
your hellos? I am
a keeper of light, invisible
dweller in the earth —
to bless me now and then
would be good, would
be wise.*

*Bless my soul!
your mother used to say.
Begin there.*

Night Sky

My closest neighbors live
half a mile away. Their lights are out.
I've returned from town
where I watched a movie with friends.
Willie, the dog my son left me
when he went away to school,
puts his wet nose on my lap
as soon as I open the truck door.

I'm glad to see him too.

He is eager to end his shift
as guard dog and go inside
to do Yoga-dog, the corpse pose,
achieving oneness with the carpet,
his four paws in the air.

Tonight, to celebrate the warm weather,
I take an outdoor pee. Willie watches me.
I wonder if I pee on my truck's hubcaps
would it confuse him, call him
to mark them again as his turf.

I linger, leaning back on the warm hood
to look at the stars. Out here, dark
means total blackness, no ambient city light,
so the huge star-mess of the Milky Way is vivid.
I locate Polaris off the Little Dipper,
then Cassiopeia, the Big Dipper,
and below it Canes Venatici, the Hunting Dogs.

This is the same sky Abraham looked up at
the night he raised his knife to slay his son Isaac.
Odysseus, Nebuchadnezzar, Ishtar, studied
this sky. Among the untold millions, each star

all by itself is or was on fire. When we look up at night,
we see a fire show.

Walking Willie to the house I stop
at the crabapple tree next to the shed.
This week its blossoms ignited all at once.
By the light of the stars it becomes
a corona of crimson, an exposed brain,
flush with blood vessels. During the day
bees work it so hard it hums
like a generator.

I snip off a flowering sprig
for a water glass in the kitchen window,
my votive offering to the stars.
The fluted O's of the flowers' mouths
will hold their dumbstruck look of awe
until they are gone.

Where do animals go when the time has come to die?

I asked my dream what it wanted,
the dream of the white pine filled
with birds: chickadees, blue jays,
house finches, red poles, a quorum
of birds holding forth in the tree,

and my dream, an old woman
awakening slowly, opening her eyes,
moving in her bed,
getting accustomed to the light,
answered me after a long interval
saying:

Sadness, remember the sadness
in the world, in other people,
the sadness of yourself, the sadness
we try to hide from ourselves,
knowing what all animals know,
that each one dies by itself,
all alone, on its own —
like those birds concealing
themselves, moving in among
the enveloping branches of the white pine, living
as if every day is their only day.

IV
Paper Rose

Paper Rose

Some mornings,
staring out my window
at the crab apple in the yard,
I give myself over to quiet,
courting its emptiness, its depths,
letting it make a claim on me,
the way it brings openness
with light around it,
one that starts small
and grows in circumference,
like the Japanese paper toy
I once had which when dropped
in a glass of water
slowly opened its cube shape,
petal by petal, into a rose.

Much passes through this circle:
faces of family, friends,
fragments from yesterday,
memories of childhood,
a snippet from *Midsummer Night's Dream*,
words, voices from the Hollywood extras
waiting their turn to appear
in my collages which form themselves
unbidden.

My father took me to a circus
in west Texas, one of those
small time outfits with just one tent,
one ring — where the clowns, sequined ladies
on horseback, trained dogs
wearing pointy hats, acrobats,
three elephants and one tired lion

jumping back and forth
through a hoop, did all their stuff
in that circle.

While laughing with Dad
at the clowns, both us us
eating cotton candy,
out of the corner of my eye
I saw my father as a boy
sitting with me, my size, tee shirt,
jeans, tennis shoes, the short haircut,
and for the first time
I realized that he too
had once been a child,
a boy, befuddled, afraid
he would never amount
to enough to please *his* father
and it was thrilling
to be there with the boy my father was,
the two of us together laughing,
cotton candy stuck to our faces,
unfolding
at the bottom of a water glass.

Circus

Next to the elephants' parade
trunks to tails, tails to trunks,
the clowns were my favorites,
their toy car whizzing around,
crazed, horn beeping, lights flashing.

It stopped in the center
of the ring and clowns blossomed
out of it like flowers
from a magician's sleeve:

one, two clowns in tall hats,
clowns three and four wearing
floppy, outlandish shoes,
fifth, sixth, seventh clowns
with drums, trombone, a tuba
clambering, birthing out
of a tiny car the size of a steamer trunk,
the eighth, ninth cavorting clowns
disgorged from the car like seeds
spit out of a milkweed pod,

and finally the world's tallest clown,
his long legs forking out of this egg
one at a time like a stork, and when
there could be no more, a midget
tumbled out, ran in circles and got back
in to drive the car away.

Dumbfounded, I asked Dad
how they did it and he explained
there was a chamber under the ring,
and a sliding door which opened
into the car parked overhead.

When I imagined them
underground, bunched together
in a colorful embroidery
of clownishness, each one
waiting his turn
to burst into the ring,
I envied them, grown men
making their living every day dressing up
in outrageous costumes,
then jumping around like fools,
without a care in the world
except how to be silly.

The Veil

Jeweler and watchmaker, my granddad
came to Kansas from Ireland, opened
a business and wore his jeweler's loop
on his forehead like a third eye.
He and the family never spoke about
the great famine.

In Costello's his tiny store in Pleasanton, Kansas
he built a three-masted schooner in a bottle
The Rose of the Sea, and kept her above
his workbench. She was tacking hard
to starboard on painted waves, her sails
billowed out in silence.

A Costello from the village of Costeloe,
tall, with a full head of white hair,
he was the family visionary with his lore,
stories, and omens. He believed in the veil,
that filmy, invisible membrane
between this world and the next,
and that it was always close.

When he walked down the sidewalk,
he seemed to move with it gracefully,
as if it were a woman on his arm.

One summer afternoon when I was
playing by myself, a silence
descended over the yard like a cloud
and my dog, the trees, even the cicadas
fell silent. For a few moments
everything in the whole neighborhood
seemed to be listening. Later, I thought
maybe it was grandfather's veil
sailing in among us like *The Rose of the Sea.*

All Souls Day, November First

This is the time of year
when the veil between worlds,
this one and the next,
is thinnest, most transparent,
and might even suddenly lift away
in certain places revealing layers
of soul beneath the tenderness
of flesh.

In my own strange underworld,
All Souls Day reminds me of Saturday
matinees at the Broadway movie theatre
in San Antonio, Texas in 1948.
I was ten and movie tickets cost
nine cents and all the kids I ever knew
and would never know were there
and we horsed around eating, laughing,
anxiously waiting for the huge purple
curtains to slowly open, and when the
house lights went down and the curtains
did open, we ran to our seats and together
stepped over the threshold of this world
into a better world, the better world
of the Bugs Bunny cartoon, the Lone Ranger
serial, and the double feature of adventure
stories spread out before us. For nine cents,
it was a great religious experience.

Today, a hundred years later, I sit in my study
at home and stare out the window at the veil time
between fall and winter, watching as geese fly
overhead in loose formations of V's (is the V
for voyage? for veil?) and the last leaves blow
off the maple trees turning this technicolor film
into black and white, and I wait for the big curtain

to open and lift revealing to me just how
imperfect and mysterious and comedic and dark
this world is, and that this world *is* the other world,
our unfathomable only-world, and how easily
any one of us might rise up from our chairs
and step into it, then wade deeply into its waters
flowing around us, cold and sweet.

Marriage Poem

When the arborist came to the house
to assess some of our trees, he carried
his long arms slightly ahead of him, and raised
as if he was ready to catch someone
falling. The stance came from the pull
and set of the powerful muscles
in his shoulders, from a lifetime of climbing
and pruning trees. He spoke of leaving school
early and I envied him his education, his
vast knowledge of trees, of something so practical.

He held the new cross leaves of the white lilac
tenderly like a boutonniere; like a father
tousling the hair of his children he ruffled
the boughs of each tree in the yard
testing their bounce and strength;
he needed to touch each tree's bark, leaves,
needles as he spoke to the tree and to me
of its history, health, and future prospects.

Like one of those long-standing,
Golden Anniversary marriages
you read about in the local paper,
his feeling for trees seemed so old and tender,
so graceful, so buried in the daily act,
I knew it would never cross his mind
to speak of it as love.

Snapshot

Mother and father, just married,
are posing for a Kodak
on the beach, their bodies
soft landscapes beneath wet swimsuits.

My brother and I are not born,
we are not contemplated, but
we are there, imponderably
within the cosmos of father's seedbag,
and the cosmos of mother's
tree of eggs.

We will be conceived and born,
we will be raised and grow into
our lives, but just then we are nowhere,
we do not exist, not even
in our parents' eyes as they look out
at the ocean, holding still
for the camera.

Maybe they are thinking
how happy they are to be alive,
to be together; maybe they were
burying their toes in the warm sand
and laughing, just before
the picture was taken.

Surely they were not thinking
that one day I would find
this photo and cherish it,
loving them and the mystery
of my brother and myself
inside them.

A Parent's Death

When my father is dying
his body lies scattered
all about him: the broken
pillars and porticos, tumbled
towers and images
of an ancient city in ruins.

A city on no map,
half-buried in the desert
perhaps at Ur,
on the Tigris and Euphrates,
the desolate landscape
where Abraham began his search
for the Promised Land.

Physicians quietly explore him,
studying his eyes, uncovering a limb,
his lower body, now pulling
the sheet back over his torso,
the way sandstorms bury and reveal
remains of a temple.
They look at me and say nothing;
he is in the final spiral.
When they do speak to me,
it is clear they know nothing.
Nor do I.

Later when you are gone,
we will tell stories about you,
your glory days, your wars,
how your lovely civilization
flourished then collapsed from within.
Some stories are true, some
we will embellish,
but we will believe them all.

Mother's Wish

is that
after an afternoon
of being taken for a drive
to see spring flowers
in yards and open fields,
trees just leafing out
against the skyline — *I love the skyline
in April, there is so much new light* —
and then to dinner
in a favorite restaurant,

she would come home
and lay her tired body
in bed, propped up
by pillows
with her ninety-year-old hands
just showing above the covers
like a child's
preparing to listen to a story,

hands with skin
so thin and transparent
her veins show through
like crisscrossing rivers
and streams seen
from a plane making
its descent,
and fall deeply asleep,
being tired from her full day,
so deep that when she awoke
she would have arrived
at the new place, having
completed her journey
in the simple, quiet style
to which she was accustomed.

Chelsea

I love those small towns
in Vermont that are tucked
inside ridge and river valley
and you come on them
around a bend
like finding a twenty
in the pocket
of some old jeans.

I just bought two work shirts
at Button's Feed Store,
where they sell socks, jackets,
boots, animal feed, dog bones,
seeds, nails, harness,
and flypaper — for starters.

It delights me — a guy
who had to wear a necktie
in school before his voice
had changed — to end up buying
my clothes in a feed store.

A cluster of fifth graders
comes down the street
as I sit on the steps
sucking on a popsicle.
They are delirious, drunk
with being nine and having money
to spend and the summer
ahead of them.

Pleasure overtakes their sentences
and they singsong, laugh-talk
at one another and wonderfully,
not a word of it is for me
or about me.

Grace

For peace to begin
it must first inhabit a quiet body,
an animal at home in its nature.

At the old well I lower a bucket
and when I bring it up
the water is beautiful, silver-bluish,
and sloshes over the sides like laughter.

This is all I am doing, my hand
on the stone rim of the well,
the water making everything
splintery glass.

I have come here, to this moment
to slow time down. At the end of my time
there will be nothing which is not
already present inside a single moment
like this one.

The closing down of the world for me
will be as simple, even as banal as the closing
of flower petals at dusk.

It is already here, I can feel it in my midst,
the ordinariness of last things.

The Dream of the Pavilion

You spend the morning
walking away from the city
into the outlands, and there
to the edge of a vast desert.

You walk into the landscape
and it is not an exhausting walk,
yes, there is sun but
there are breezes too,
and you have water and your map.

Toward the afternoon
you see in the distance
a canvas structure, a pavilion
with four flags positioned
at its corners, near an oasis:
water and trees and this blue
canvas tent with its white flags.

You approach the shelter
with caution and some fear
but when you open the flap
there is no one there, so
you enter and sit down.

All night you sit in the tent
listening to the sounds the flags
make in the wind: the sound
of laughter, of water over stones,
and later the sound of your heart.

When morning comes you leave
the pavilion with its flags, returning
to the city and your life there,
but in its four chambers
your heart keeps the memory.

Notes

The names in the hospital poems are all fictional.

STAT is hospital code for: *very urgent / crisis call.*

The Caul is for Eileen Reynolds.

About the Author

Tom Absher recently retired after forty years of college teaching in Literature and Creative Writing. Most of his teaching was done at Goddard College and Vermont College. He received a Ph.D. from the University of Pennsylvania in the English Renaissance and an M.F.A. in Poetry from Goddard College. Over the years he was awarded two National Endowment for the Arts Fellowships in poetry and a grant from the Vermont Council on the Arts. He was a YMHA/Nation Discovery Award winner and received a Dana grant for creative writing from Norwich University. He has three other books of poetry, *Forms of Praise*, Ohio State University Press, *The Calling*, AliceJames Books, and *The Invisible Boy*, The Writers Voice, and a book of essays, *Men and the Goddess*, Park Street Press. He, Erika Butler, and their two cats, Fergus and Maeve, live in rural Vermont.

www.ingramcontent.com/pod-product-compliance
Lightning Source LLC
Chambersburg PA
CBHW071027080526
44587CB00015B/2529